AF457150

Table of Contents

INTRODUCTION TO CYBER SECURITY

Cyber security is the application of technologies, processes and controls to protect systems, networks, programs, devices and data from cyber attacks. It aims to reduce the risk of cyber attacks and protect against the unauthorised exploitation of systems, networks and technologies

What is Cyber security

Cyber security is the practice of defending computers, servers, mobile devices, electronic systems, networks, and data from malicious attacks. It's also known as information technology security or electronic information security.

NETWORK SECURITY

Network security is a technique that enables organizations to secure computer networks from intruders, targeted attackers, and opportunistic malware. As the Internet has an assortment of networks associated with various websites, it is often observed that the organizations become targeted with unauthorized intrusion, with malicious intent. Also, as many websites contain third party cookies, the users' activities are tracked. Sometimes this might prove helpful for organizations to grow their businesses, but often customers become prey to fraud and sexual exploitation. Hence to counter the cyber attacks and malware associated with the network, organizations must deploy a security program to monitor the internal network and infrastructure. Experts have suggested leveraging Machine learning technology that will alert the authorities in case of abnormal traffic. The organizations must continue to upgrade their network security by implementing policies that can thwart cyber-attacks.

Experts suggest the following methods for upgraded network security:

- Extra Logins
- New Passwords
- Antivirus programs
- Firewalls

- Incognito Mode

- Monitored Internet access

- Encryption

APPLICATION SECURITY

Application security focuses on keeping software and devices free of threats. A compromised application could provide access to the data its designed to protect. Successful security begins in the design stage, The users get infatuated with different applications, which include hardware, software, and devices. But an application becomes equally prone to cyber-attack or malware like the network. Application security thwarts the cyber-security infringement by adopting the hardware and software methods at the development phase of the project. With the help of an application security network, the companies and organizations can detect the sensitive data set and secure them with specific applications about the datasets.

Some of the methods associated with application security are:

- Anti-virus Program
- Firewalls
- Encryption Programs

CRITICAL INFRASTRUCTURE CYBER SECURITY

Critical infrastructure cyber-security technique is deployed to secure the systems that have the critical infrastructure. They are systems on which the societies heavily rely on. These include- Electricity grid, Water Purification, Traffic lights, Shopping centers, and hospitals. They are not directly linked with a possible cyber infringement but can act as a platform through which the cyber malware can happen to the endpoints that these systems are connected to. To mitigate the possibility of cyber malware or reduce cyber attacks, the organizations responsible for maintaining critical infrastructure must access the vulnerable points for protecting the businesses that they are liable with. Organizations that utilize the critical infrastructure must also evaluate the amount of damage caused due to cyber attacks. These organizations must have a contingency plan that would help their businesses to bear no brunt of the cyber attacks.

CLOUD SECURITY

Most of the organizations are now inclined towards utilizing artificial intelligence to improve their businesses, enhance customer experience, and for efficient operations. With the plethora of data available at each step of organizational set-up, it becomes difficult for organizations to store these data in physical form. Also, it is observed that often this data is unstructured and is derived from unknown sources, which can cause a potential threat to the organization's network. Hence, Amazon Web Services, Microsoft Azure, and Google Cloud present their customers with a cloud computing platform, where the users can store, and monitor data, by implementing a security tool. Report suggest that on-premise environments are highly prone to cyber malware. By integrating the system with a cloud security platform, the users will be rendered with the secured data, thus mitigating the possibility of a cyber-attack.

THE INTERNET OF THINGS SECURITY

The Internet of things is being observed to be the next tool for the technological revolution. A report by Bain and Company has estimated the market size for IoT to expand by US$520 billion by the year 2021. With the help of
its security Network. IcT provides the user with a variety of critical and non critical appliances such as the appliances, sensors, printers, and wifi-routers amongst routers. The report suggests that one of the main obstacles for implementing

IoT in any organization is the threat to security. By integrating the system with IoT security, organizations are provided with insightful analytics, legacy embedded systems, and secure network.

OPERATIONAL SECURITY

Operational security (OPSEC), also known as procedural security, is a risk management process that encourages managers to view operations from the perspective of an adversary in order to protect sensitive information from falling into the wrong hands. The permissions users have when accessing a network and the procedures that determine how and where data may be stored or shared all fall under this umbrella. Things that fall under the OPSEC umbrella also include monitoring behaviors and habits on social media sites as well as discouraging employees from sharing login credentials via email or text message.

THE FIVE STEPS OF OPERATIONAL SECURITY

The processes involved in operational security can be neatly categorized into five steps:

Identify your sensitive data.

This include your product research, intellectual property, financial statements, customer information, and employee information. This will be the data you will need to focus your resources on protecting.

Identify possible threats.

For each category of information that you deem sensitive, you should identify what kinds of threats are present. While you should be wary of third parties trying to steal your information, you should also watch out for insider threats, such as negligent employees and disgruntled workers.

Analyze security holes and other vulnerabilities.

Assess your current safeguards and determine what, if any, loopholes or weaknesses exist that may be exploited to gain access to your sensitive data.

Appraise the level of risk associated with each vulnerability.

Rank your vulnerabilities using factors such as the likelihood of an attack happening, the extent of damage that you would suffer, and the amount of work and time you would need to recover. The more likely and damaging an attack is, the more you should prioritize mitigating the associated risk.

Get countermeasures in place.

The last step of operational security is to create and implement a plan to eliminate threats and mitigate risks. This could include updating your hardware, creating new policies regarding sensitive data, or training employees on sound security practices and company policies.

Countermeasures should be straightforward and simple. Employees should be able to implement the measures required on their part with or without additional training.

WHY IS CYBER SECURITY IMPORTANT

Rise of Cyber Crimes

Be it a large scale or a small scale firm, hackers and cyber criminals spare no one. Rather, they lookout for opportunities to exploit data and get money out of these firms. Over the past year, the average cost of cyber crime for an organization has increased 23% more than last year—US$11.7 million, according to the report. Also, the average number of security breaches has risen significantly and it is now $3.86 million, as per the report. With the introduction of new technologies, the chances of cyber threats and risks are also rapidly increasing. Cyber criminals have advanced their attempts of deploying cyber attacks with the evolution of technology.

Growth of IoT Devices

With the mission to create smart cities with smart devices, our dependency to connect everything to the internet has increased too. The introduction of IoT technology i.e. Internet of Things, has not only simplified and speed up our tasks but has also created a pit of new vulnerabilities for hackers to exploit. No matter how advanced security measures we take, cyber criminals will always stay one step ahead to attempt cyber crimes. If these internet-connected devices are not managed properly then they can provide a gateway to business to hackers or cyber criminals!

Bridge to Security Gap

Human resources and IT resources have always been one of the most important aspects of any organization. Regardless of their dependency on each other, there has always been a security gap between both aspects. In order to bridge this gap, it is important to provide individuals working in an organization with the right cyber security awareness training. Training for employees is necessary to bridge the gap of cyber security skills and to create a cyber-resilient working culture in the organization.

Cost of Cyber Risks

Cyber attacks today are not only multiplying in numbers but are also multiplying in the cost of damage created. These cyber attacks can prove to be extremely expensive for any organization to endure if not taken proper security measures. With more business infrastructures connecting, it is predicted, cyber crime to cost the world $10.5 trillion annually by 2025, says the report. Besides, it is not just the financial damage that could cost but also the reputation of the firm along with loss of customer trust in the business.

Security of Data

When it comes to data security, it can be clearly seen how organizations are getting highly comfortable in keeping their information online. With the alarming number of data breaches and information leaks making news headlines almost every day, it can be seen how vulnerable the data left is online. Moreover, cyber attack vectors such as ransomware, phishing, cyber scams, risk of removable media, etc. leave no room for data exploitation and publicizing of any vulnerable data. Implementation of the right cyber security solutions is a must to avoid any future cyber risks related to the sensitive data of an organization.

It protects all categories of data from theft and damage.

This includes sensitive data, personally identifiable information (PII), protected health information (PHI), personal information, intellectual property, data, and governmental and industry information systems. Without a cybersecurity program, your organization cannot defend itself against data breach campaigns, making it an irresistible target for cybercriminals.

Some Elements Of Cybercrime.

1. Cybercrime includes single actors or groups targeting systems for financial gain or to cause disruption.

2. Cyber-attack often involves politically motivated information gathering.

3. Cyberterrorism is intended to undermine electronic systems to cause panic or fear.

Things about Cyber Security You Need to Know.

Most modern businesses have incorporated cyber security solutions into their operations to increase efficiency. In general, administrative, accounting, marketing, communication and clerical tasks in companies are being performed on digital platforms. This shift has notable advantages, including that it's faster, usage of few paper resources and effective collaboration between employees. As a result, numerous enterprises have managed to increase their productivity and revenue and reduce losses related to common inefficiencies. On the other hand, the use of IT for the management of company data and processes presents a significant risk for businesses. There are numerous threats which can compromise the digital platform. In simple terms, corporations and organizations with IT hackers and other malicious characters frequently attacking setups. This often leads to loss of critical data, business continuity compromise, financial expenses and loss of customer trust. The increase in commercial network threats has led to a higher demand for professionals with cyber security knowledge and skills. This field is focused on detecting, preventing and managing the threats on digital platforms. The responsibilities will also encompass setting up security measures and performing regular monitoring of network activities. Most people who work in this field earn at least a bachelor's degree in cybersecurity or a similar field. They need specialized knowledge to help stop hackers and repair the damage done to systems.

Here are the ten factors you need to know

Most cyber threats can be prevented.

There are numerous reports on companies, which have been attacked by hackers and lost significant revenue. While these threats look complex and sophisticated to an inexperienced eye, most of them can be presented by establishing the right security measures.

Poor email security poses major threats.

One of the main causes of poor company security is email messages. Often, malicious people will send phishing emails, which attempt to obtain confidential company information by installing malware into the network or redirecting to compromised domains.

Mobile phones can cause security breaches.

More companies are relying on mobile devices such as smartphones and tablets to perform operations out of the office. While this is efficient, a device without the right protective measures can be easily compromised through theft or hacking.

IcT will present new security challenges.

The future of the business world is in the Internet of Things (IoT), which seeks to interconnect all digital resources. This integration will improve efficiency, but great expertise will be required to handle the new threats.

Most companies avoid encryption.

Encryption is a well-known concept which is designed to prevent outsiders from reading confidential data if they do access it. Unfortunately, most companies favor this security measure but they have not implemented it into their organizations.

Attacks cause loss of customer trust.

When hackers attack a company, the customers tend to lose trust in them. This is particularly true for enterprises, which are entrusted with financial information. Therefore, even if the company recovers their information, recovering their customer's trust will be more difficult.

Downtime can cripple businesses.

Cyber-attacks cause downtime in business. A normal company will take time away to regroup and restore the systems. The downtime can be crippling because the time taken will allow customers to shift their attention to competitors.

Employee negligence can compromise network security.

The most significant cyber threats come from hackers and their malicious software. However, employee negligence can contribute to the loss of data and security breaches. This aspect should be accounted for when setting up cyber security measures.

IT security intelligence is underutilized.

Intelligence on cyber security threats is available on numerous platforms with IT professionals. However, this information is not utilized in most companies because technicians are unaware. As a potential specialist, you should know the importance of being aware.

There is cyber security skills shortage.

While most businesses are using IT for daily tasks, numerous companies lack professionals to handle their security. This can be attributed to the shortage of cyber security experts.

What Is a Cyber Security Threat?

A cyber security threat refers to any possible malicious attack that seeks to unlawfully access data, disrupt digital operations or damage information. Cyber threats can originate from various actors, including corporate spies, hacktivists, terrorist groups, hostile nation-states, criminal organizations, lone hackers and disgruntled employees. In recent years, numerous high-profile cyber attacks have resulted in sensitive data being exposed. For example, the 2017 Equifax breach compromised the personal data of roughly 143 million consumers, including birth dates, addresses and Social Security numbers. In 2018, Marriott International disclosed that hackers accessed its servers and stole the data of roughly 500 million customers. In both instances, the cyber security threat was enabled by the organization's failure to implement, test and retest technical safeguards, such as encryption, authentication and firewalls. Cyber attackers can use an individual's or a company's sensitive data to steal information or gain access to their financial accounts, among other potentially damaging actions, which is why cyber security professionals are essential for keeping private data protected.

7 Types of Cyber Security Threats

Cyber security professionals should have an in-depth understanding of the following types of cyber security threats.

Malware

Malware is malicious software such as spyware, ransomware, viruses and worms. Malware is activated when a user clicks on a malicious link or attachment, which leads to installing dangerous software. Cisco reports that malware, once activated, can:

Block access to key network components (ransomware)

Install additional harmful software

Covertly obtain information by transmitting data from the hard drive (spyware)

There are a number of different types of malware, including:

· Virus: A self-replicating program that attaches itself to clean file and spreads throughout a computer system, infecting files with malicious code.

· Trojans: A type of malware that is disguised as legitimate software. Cybercriminals trick users into uploading Trojans onto their computer where they cause damage or collect data.

· Spyware: A program that secretly records what a user does, so that cybercriminals can make use of this information. For example, spyware could capture credit card details.

· Ransomware: Malware which locks down a user’s files and data, with the threat of erasing it unless a ransom is paid.

· Adware: Advertising software which can be used to spread malware.

· Botnets: Networks of malware infected computers which cybercriminals use to perform tasks online without the user's permission.

Emotet

The Cybersecurity and Infrastructure Security Agency (CISA) describes Emotet as "an advanced, modular banking Trojan that primarily functions as a downloader or dropper of other banking Trojans. Emotet continues to be among the most costly and destructive malware."

Denial of Service

A denial of service (DoS) is a type of cyber attack that floods a computer or network so it can’t respond to requests.

A distributed DoS (DDoS) does the same thing, but the attack originates from a computer network. Cyber attackers often use a flood attack to disrupt the “handshake” process and carry out a DoS. Several other techniques may be used, and some cyber attackers use the time that a network is disabled to launch other attacks.

A botnet is a type of DDoS in which millions of systems can be infected with malware and controlled by a hacker, according to Jeff Melnick of Netwrix, an information technology security software company. Botnets, sometimes called zombie systems, target and overwhelm a target's processing capabilities. Botnets are in different geographic locations and hard to trace.

Man in the Middle attack

A man-in-the-middle (MITM) attack occurs when hackers insert themselves into a two-party transaction. After interrupting the traffic, they can filter and steal data, according to Cisco. MITM attacks often occur when a visitor uses an unsecured public Wi-Fi network. Attackers insert themselves between the visitor and the network, and then use malware to install software and use data maliciously.

Phishing

Phishing attacks use fake communication, such as an email, to trick the receiver into opening it and carrying out the instructions inside, such as providing a credit card number. “The goal is to steal sensitive data like credit card and login information or to install malware on the victim’s machine,” Cisco reports.

SQL Injection

A Structured Query Language (SQL) injection is a type of cyber attack that results from inserting malicious code into a server that uses SQL. When infected, the server releases information. Submitting the malicious code can be as simple as entering it into a vulnerable website search box. This gives them access to the sensitive information contained in the database.

Password Attacks

With the right password, a cyber attacker has access to a wealth of information. Social engineering is a type of password attack that Data Insider defines as "a strategy cyber attackers use that relies heavily on human interaction and often involves tricking people into breaking standard security practices." Other types of password attacks include accessing a password database or outright guessing.

Protect yourself against cyberattacks

How can businesses and individuals guard against cyber threats? Here are some top cyber safety tips.

1. Update your software and operating system: This means you benefit from the latest security patches.

2. Use anti-virus software: Security solutions like Kaspersky Total Securitywill detect and removes threats. Keep your software updated for the best level of protection.

3. Use strong passwords: Ensure your passwords are not easily guessable.

4. Do not open email attachments from unknown senders: These could be infected with malware.

5. Do not click on links in emails from unknown senders or unfamiliar websites:This is a common way that malware is spread.

6. Avoid using unsecure WiFi networks in public places: Unsecure networks leave you vulnerable to man-in-the-middle attacks.

EVOLUTION OF CYBER SECURITY

Cyber security practices continue to evolve as the internet and digitally dependent operations develop and change. According to Secureworks, people who study cyber security are turning more of their attention to the two areas in the following sections.

1. The Internet of Things

Individual devices that connect to the internet or other networks offer an access point for hackers.

Cytelligence reports that in 2019, hackers increasingly targeted smart home and internet of things (IoT) devices, such as smart TVs, voice assistants, connected baby monitors and cellphones. Hackers who successfully compromise a connected home not only gain access to users' Wi-Fi credentials, but may also gain access to their data, such as medical records, bank statements and website login information.

2. The Explosion of Data

Data storage on devices such as laptops and cellphones makes it easier for cyber attackers to find an entry point into a network through a personal device. For example, in the May 2019 book Exploding Data: Reclaiming Our Cyber Security in the Digital Age, former U.S. Secretary of Homeland Security Michael Chertoff warns of a pervasive exposure of individuals' personal information, which has become increasingly vulnerable to cyber attacks.

Consequently, companies and government agencies need

maximum cyber security to protect their data and operations. Understanding how to address the latest evolving cyber threats is essential for cyber security professionals.

The Top Skills Required for Cybersecurity Jobs

1. Problem-Solving Skills

As a cybersecurity professional, problem-solving will play a major role in your day-to-day work. Those in the field need to find creative ways to take on and address complex information security challenges across a variety of existing and emerging technologies and digital environments.

2. Technical Aptitude

As the name implies, cybersecurity is a technology-focused field: you will be likely be tasked with responsibilities such as troubleshooting, maintaining, and updating information security systems; implementing continuous network monitoring; and providing real-time security solutions. Being technologically savvy is essential in order to perform the daily activities of a cybersecurity professional.

3. Knowledge of Security Across Various Platforms

Cybersecurity isn't just limited to computers: you'll need to be comfortable working on a variety of operating systems, computer systems, mobile devices, cloud networks, and wireless networks - and keep up to date on advances in the field for all of them.

4. Attention to Detail

Being able to defend an organization against cyber

breaches requires you to be highly vigilant and detail-oriented, in order to effectively detect vulnerabilities and risks. You'll like be responsible for continuous network monitoring and will need to be able to quickly identify concerns and come up with real-time security solutions to address them.

5. Communication Skills

As a cybersecurity specialist, you'll be working closely with individuals in other roles and departments, and it's important to be able to effectively communicate and explain your findings, concerns, and solutions to others. It's important to be able to speak clearly and concisely on cybersecurity strategy and policy, as well as to be able to convey technical information to individuals of different levels of technical comprehension.

6. Fundamental Computer Forensics Skills

While computer forensics and cybersecurity are two separate fields, they're closely related - and having a foundation in computer forensics can help you excel in your cybersecurity career. To be able to effectively protect organizations' digital assets and prevent security breaches, you'll need to have a solid understanding of what happens if your efforts fail, and how compromised data is recovered. Most cybersecurity degree programs will have a computer forensics component for this reason.

7. A Desire to Learn

As with any technical field, cybersecurity is fast-changing. Anyone who works in the field will need to be committed to keeping current with best practices and emerging industry trends, and will always need to be learning and self-educating - both on and off the clock.

8. An Understanding of Hacking

To effectively protect an organization's network and infrastructure, you'll need to know how they can be exploited in the first place - that's why most cybersecurity professionals must learn how to "ethically hack." Essentially, you need to have the same skills as a hacker, to fully understand how a system could be breached, and in turn, create effective solutions for thwarting these attacks.

How Do You Build Cybersecurity Skills?

While some of the skills listed above are ones you should naturally have - for example, an inclination for analytical thinking and technology - others are ones you will need to develop through formal training or education. Depending on your background, a certificate or degree in cybersecurity is a good place to start: they'll give you a solid foundation in the principles of cybersecurity, in addition to an overview of security across a variety of platforms, programming and development, digital forensic investigation, specific technical skills (such as those relating to computer and operating systems and networking) and more. Given the growing popularity of this field, there are an increasing number of cybersecurity degree programs available to prospective students, both online and campus-based. Regardless of the mode of learning you prefer, you should look for a school that is regionally accredited, non-profit, and has a well-recognized cybersecurity program. Third-party validation from both the higher education industry (for example, U.S. News & World Report rankings) and the cybersecurity industry (such as SC Magazine's rankings) are important.

Solid Work Habits

First, you'll need some essential work habits, including the ability to work methodically (and in a detail-oriented way). The following abilities also come in useful:

Eagerness to dig into technical questions and examine them from all sides.

Enthusiasm and a high degree of adaptability.

Strong analytical and diagnostic skills.

A current understanding of common web vulnerabilities.

Maintaining awareness and knowledge of contemporary

standards, practices, procedures and methods.

Soft Skills

That's in addition to the aforementioned soft skills; remember, security professionals often need to communicate complicated subjects to people who might not have much of a technical background (such as C-suite executives).

With that in mind, mastering the following is usually a perquisite for climbing to more advanced positions on the cybersecurity ladder:

Excellent presentation and communications skills to effectively communicate with management and customers.

Ability to clearly articulate complex concepts (both written and verbally).

Ability, understanding, and usage of active listening skills (especially with customers!).

From a cybersecurity perspective, soft skills will also allow you to identify examples of, and explain, social engineering, which is a pervasive issue within the security community. You can put all kinds of hardware and software security measures in place, but hackers can still use social engineering to convince unsuspecting employees to give them passwords, credentials, and access to otherwise-secure systems.

Technical Skills

Which technical skills do cybersecurity pros need? That question is a bit trickier to answer, as there are many sub-disciplines within the cybersecurity field. That being said, many such jobs share a common technical foundation.

For starters, tech pros should understand the architecture, administration, and management of operating systems (various Linux distros, Windows, etc.), networking, and virtualization software. In other words, get to know—and love—things like firewalls and network load balancers. That's in addition to general programming/software development concepts and software analytics skills.

There's also the need to understand the more common programming languages, including Java, C/C++, disassemblers, assembly language, and scripting languages (PHP, Python, Perl, or shell).

Many employers demand certifications as a perquisite for employment, and it’s easy to see why. In a recent survey, the International Information System Security Certification Consortium (ISC)^2 noted that a degree and certifications were often a major factor in hiring. “Cybersecurity certifications are essential to showing the level of knowledge of a cybersecurity professional. However, they should never alone be the only reference,”

Implementation Skills

Any good cybersecurity pro knows how to examine a company's security setup from a holistic view, including threat modeling, specifications, implementation, testing, and vulnerability assessment. They also understand security issues associated with operating systems, networking, and virtualization software.

But it's not just about understanding; it's also about implementation. They study the architecture of systems and networks, then use that information to identify the security controls in place and how they are used. Same with weaknesses in databases and app deployment.

More junior cybersecurity professionals might use their coding skills to write tools that automate certain security tasks; depending on the company's technology stack, there is often a choice of pre-built tools that will automate many functions, as well.

Management Skills

Senior cybersecurity pros, meanwhile, must organize and coordinate technical vulnerability assessments, including systems and network vulnerability assessments, penetration testing, web application assessments, social engineering assessments, physical security assessments, wireless security assessments and implementing secure infrastructure solutions.

They recommend and set the technical direction for managing security incidents, and ensure the integrity of the resulting process and approach. In terms of using soft skills, they'll need to explain to management (and show forensically) how an attack was conducted.

Words Related to Cyber Security.

- Disaster Recovery and Business Continuity define how an organization responds to a cyber-security incident or any other event that causes the loss of operations or datta. Disaster recovery policies dictate how the organization restores its operations and information to return to the same operating capacity as before the event.

Business continuity is the plan the organization falls back on while trying to operate without certain resources.

- End-User Education addresses the most unpredictable cyber-security factor: people. Anyone can accidentally introduce a virus to an otherwise secure system by failing to follow good security practices. Teaching users to delete suspicious email attachments, not plug in unidentified USB drives, and various other important lessons is vital for the security of any organization.

- End-User Protection or Endpoint Security is a crucial aspect of cyber security. After all, it is often an individual (the end-user) who accidentally uploads malware or another form of cyber threat to their desktop, laptop or mobile device.

So, how do cyber-security measures protect end users and systems? First, cyber-security relies on cryptographic protocols to encrypt emails, files, and other critical data. This can only protects information in transit, but also guards against loss or theft.

In addition, end-user security software scans computers for pieces of malicious code, quarantines this code, and then removes it from the machine. Security programs can even detect and remove malicious code hidden in primary boot record and are designed to encrypt or wipe data from computer's hard drive.

- Electronic Security protocols also focus on real-time malware detection. Many use heuristic and behavioral analysis to monitor the behavior of a program and its code to defend against viruses or Trojans that change their shape with each execution (polymorphic and metamorphic malware).

- Security programs can confine potentially malicious programs to a virtual bubble separate from a user's network to analyze their behavior and learn how to better detect new infections.

Security programs continue to evolve new defenses as cyber-security professionals identify new threats and new ways to combat them. To make the most of end-user security software, employees need to be educated about how to use it. Crucially, keeping it running and updating it frequently ensures that it can protect users against the latest cyber threats.

How to Protect your Organization Against Cybercrime

There are three simple steps you can take you to increase security and reduce risk of cybercrime:

1. Educate Staff

Human error was the cause of 90% of data breaches in 2019. This concerning statistic, however, has a silver lining. If staff are taught how to identify and correctly respond to cyber threats, the majority of data breach incidents could be avoided. Such educational programs could also increase the value of all cybersecurity solution investments because it would prevent staff from unknowingly bypassing expensive security.

Employees who are untrained in proper security practices are a huge vulnerability. It's absolutely critical to train employees to recognize warning signs of cybercrime, as well as how to keep risks low in the first place, and there should be a system in place for reporting signs of an attack.

2. Create a system security plan

A system security plan (SSP) is a summary of all security practices that keep your data secure. The SSP identifies features in a system such as hardware, software, security measures, training methods and incident-response plans.

This document includes details on how to limit access to authorized users and ensure employees practice secure habits and respond in the case of a security breach. It also prevents things from falling through the cracks when schedules get busy. If your IT staff is knowledgeable on this subject, you can save money by keeping things in-house, but otherwise, it's better to hire a consultant. A badly written SSP could end up costing you more in the end.

3. Keep software updated

Many SMBs get too busy to ensure their software is updated in a timely manner, but outdated software can expose your company to vulnerable security flaws. Hackers often study the latest software updates in order to target those businesses who are behind in adopting them. According to Fortinet's 2017 Global Threat Landscape report, 60 percent of organized security breaches targeted vulnerabilities that were at least 10 years old.

4. Enforce secure password policies

Passwords should never be recycled, and they should be updated constantly. Simple passwords are also easy for hackers to crack. In 2012, a password-cracking expert revealed a program that could work around any eight-character password. This is why all passwords should be more than eight characters, and the more complicated, the better.

5. Outsource cybersecurity

There are many resources you can turn to if you feel overwhelmed at the thought of managing cybersecurity issues yourself. Many small companies decide to put cybersecurity at the back of their mind because they don't understand it. Doing this could be your downfall, though.

Many IT companies specialize in helping small businesses improve their security. Sometimes an even simpler option is to use anti-malware or anti-ransomware technology. According to done by Verizon, 28 percent of security breaches involve malware. By using a software program that prevents malware attacks, you can significantly lower your security risks.

Running an SMB is a stressful, time-consuming endeavor,
so avoid the temptation to place cybersecurity on your company's backburner. Starting today, make your business's online security a conscious priority and you'll be primed for sucess (and fewer headaches) in the long run.

6. Data back-up

Backing up data is among the most cost-effective ways of making sure information is recovered in an event of a cyber incident or computer issues. The department recommended using multiple back-up methods to help ensure data safety, including daily incremental back-ups to a portable device or cloud storage, and end-of-week, quarterly, and yearly server back-ups. Backed up data should also be checked regularly to see if it is working properly and can be restored.

As for portable devices, the department said they should not be left connected to a computer to prevent infection and should be stored separately offsite as protection from theft and other physical damage. Cloud storage, meanwhile, should use strong encryption methods and multi-factor authentication to ensure data protection.

7. Securing network and data

Operating systems and security software should be updated automatically to fix security flaws, so it is important that users never disregard update prompts, according to the bureau. Firewalls should also be set up as these act as a "gatekeeper for all incoming and outgoing traffic." It would also be helpful for companies to turn on spam filters to reduce the amount of spam and phishing emails – a common tactic hackers use to infect devices and steal confidential information – that their businesses receive.

8. Activate data encryption

Encryption converts data into a secret code before it is sent over the internet, so it is vital for businesses to turn on network and data encryption when storing and sharing data. This can be activated through router settings or by installing a virtual private network (VPN) software on computers and other devices.

9. Use multi-factor authentication

Another standard practice to protect data is the use of multi-factor authentication (MFA). This verification process requires users to provide two or more proofs of their identities to access their accounts, adding another layer of security. One example is a system where a password and a code sent to a separate device are required before a user is granted access to an online account.

10. Replace passwords with passphrases

It is better you use passphrases instead of passwords, especially for accounts that hold important business information. A secure passphrase should be at least 14 characters long, and consists of a combination of upper and lower case letters, numbers, and special characters. It should also be unpredictable – meaning the words are unrelated – and unique – meaning it is not used for other accounts.

11. Comprehensive monitoring system

A business should keep a record of all the equipment and software it uses. It should remove sensitive information from any device and software that is no longer in use and disconnect these devices from its network. The bureau said older and unused equipment or software will unlikely be updated and may serve as a "backdoor targeted by criminals to attack businesses." Similarly, organisations should remove access from past employees and those who have changed roles and no longer require access.

12. Implement security policies

Businesses should also have clear cybersecurity policies to guide employees on what is acceptable when sharing data, using computers and other devices, and accessing internet sites

Why is Cybercrime Increasing?

Information theft is the most expensive and fastest-growing segment of cybercrime. Largely driven by the increasing exposure of identity information to the web via cloud services. But it's not the only target. Industrial controls that manage power grids and other infrastructure can be disrupted or destroyed. And identity theft isn't the only goal, cyber attacks may aim to compromise data integrity (destroy or change data) to breed distrust in an organization or government. Cybercriminals are becoming more sophisticated, changing what they target, how they affect organizations and their methods of attack for different security systems. Social engineering remains the easiest form of cyber attack with ransomware, phishing, and spywarebeing the easiest form of entry. Third-party and fourth-party vendors who process your data and have poor cybersecurity practices are another common attack vector, making vendor risk management and third-party risk management all the more important. According to the Ninth

Annual Cost of Cybercrime Study from Accenture and the Ponemon Institute, the average cost of cybercrime for an organization has increased by $1.4 million over the last year to $13.0 million and the average number of data breaches rose by 11 percent to 145. Information risk managementhas never been more important. Data breaches can involve financial information like credit card numbers or bank account details, protected health information (PHI), personally identifiable information (PII), trade secrets, intellectual property and other targets of industrial espionage. Other terms for data breaches include unintentional information disclosure, data leak, cloud leak, information leakage or a data spill. Other factors driving the growth in cybercrime include: The distributed nature of the Internet The ability for cybercriminals to attack targets outside their jurisdiction making policing extremely difficult Increasing profitability and ease of commerce on the dark web The proliferation of mobile devices and the Internet of Things.

What is the Impact of Cybercrime?

A lack of focus on cybersecurity can damage your business in range of ways including:

1. Economic Costs

Theft of intellectual property, corporate information, disruption in trading and the cost of repairing damaged systems

2. Reputational Cost

Loss of consumer trust, loss of current and future customers to competitors and poor media coverage

3. Regulatory Costs

GDPR and other data breach laws mean that your organization could suffer from regulatory fines or sanctions as a result of cybercrimes.

All businesses, regardless of the size, must ensure all staff understand cybersecurity threats and how to mitigate them. This should include regular training and a framework to work with to that aims to reduce the risk of data leaks or data breaches.

Given the nature of cybercrime and how difficult it can be to detect, it is difficult to understand the direct and indirect costs of many security breaches. This doesn't mean the reputational damage of even a small data breach or other security event is not large. If anything, consumers expect increasingly sophisticated cybersecurity measures as time goes on.

MOST FREQUENTLY ASKED QUESTIONS

WHAT TYPES OF BUSINESSES ARE MOST AT RISK FOR A CYBERATTACK?

You may think that big businesses with more endpoints are more vulnerable than small businesses. Or, businesses with attractive data, like financial services companies or those in the healthcare industry, would be easy targets. That's not always the case—of course, they hold an incredible amount of data, but it's like trying to rob the

Federal Reserve gold vault versus robbing a regular Joe on the street. Bigger businesses or those that handle sensitive data typically have the technology, regulations, and processes to protect themselves from cyberattacks. On the other hand, small and medium-sized businesses without dedicated IT expertise, cybersecurity technology, processes, or education are easy targets for hackers.

WHAT'S ONE OF THE BIGGEST CYBERSECURITY CHALLENGES BUSINESSES FACE?

One of the biggest challenges currently facing businesses is staying educated when it comes to cybersecurity and being aware of evolving cyberthreats. Most often, hackers initiate cyberattacks after finding a way to steal an employee's username and password. We use "steal" lightly—hackers typically trick users into handing their information over. Once the hacker gains access to the system, they can sit back and wait until they have a perfect, lucrative opportunity to execute an attack. With proper cybersecurity education and best practices in place, businesses can help protect themselves from the most commonly executed information hacks and cyberattacks. One of the most effective forms of cybersecurity education is Security Awareness Training — learn more about it here.

ARE ORGANIZATIONS DOING ENOUGH TO COMBAT CYBERTHREATS?

In most cases, the simple answer is no.

Cybersecurity requires consistent education, company-wide processes, and executive-level commitment. Generally, there needs to be more awareness surrounding how quickly hackers can initiate a cyberattack, how quickly cyberattacks evolve, and how businesses need multiple layers of cybersecurity to protect themselves—especially in modern workplace environments where employees are working remotely and sharing a ton of important data via digital communication channels.

WHAT ARE THE MOST CONCERNING CYBERTHREATS RIGHT NOW?

Ransomware is one of our biggest concerns—it's a specific type of cyberattack where hackers deploy malware, then force you to pay a ransom in order to regain access to your system—more on ransomware below. We're also always concerned with monitoring and preventing lateral phishing takeover attacks. Through these types of cyberattacks, hackers gain access to an employee's email account. Then, they set up rules to extract valuable data and information. Once hackers find a piece of information they can exploit, they use it to create a genuine-looking email to everyone in the employee's address book. With advanced technologies and machine learning, hackers can make phishing emails look frighteningly legitimate. As other employees open and interact with the email, hackers gain access to more data and information until the entire organization is potentially affected.

WHAT ARE SOME COMMON TYPES OF COMPUTER VIRUSES?

Common examples of computer viruses include resident viruses, multipartite viruses, direct actions, browser hijackers, overwrite viruses, web scripting viruses, file injectors, network viruses, and boot sector viruses. Here's a full list of common computer viruses, including how to recognize them and common symptoms of a virus attack.

WHAT IS MALWARE

Malware, short for malicious software, is a program or file that is intentionally harmful to your computer, network, or website. These types of cyberthreats infect your system to gather sensitive data, disrupt operations, or spy on your digital activity. Common examples of malware include viruses, ransomware, Trojans, spyware, keyloggers, and worms.

WHAT IS RANSOMWARE?

Ransomware is a specific type of cyberattack where the attacker forces you to pay a ransom fee to regain access to your system or files. Common types of ransomware attacks include scareware, lock-screen ransomware, and encryption ransomware. We outline everything you need to know about ransomware here, including how to protect yourself from ransomware attacks and what you should do if you fall victim to ransomware.

HOW DO YOU BUILD A CYBERSECURITY SOLUTION?

Cybersecurity isn't a one-size-fits-all product. Businesses need to take a layered approach to cybersecurity for defense, monitoring, and remediation. The specific solution you need for your business will be a combination of firewalls, email security, anti-virus, patching, VPN connections, endpoint protection, multifactor authentication, user education and security awareness training (SAT), endpoint detection and response (EDR), security information and event management (SIEM), and data backup. Learn more about the 11 layers that make up a comprehensive cybersecurity solution.

HOW CAN WE BUILD A SAFER CYBERWORLD?

It all comes down to education, processes, and technology. Businesses need to invest in educating employees on cybersecurity best practices. Additionally, businesses need to effectively secure the data they've been entrusted with. Users, internal and external, should make more informed decisions when interacting with technology.

WHAT SHOULD I DO IF I SUSPECT A CYBERATTACK?

Your organization should have a cyberattack remediation process in place. If you're unsure, ask your IT provider or someone in your internal IT department—it could save your business money and its reputation if a cyberattack occurs.

HOW MUCH DOES CYBERSECURITY COST?

As much as we'd love to throw a perfectly round number out there, it's tough. Cybersecurity solutions really depend on your organization's individual needs. Once we determine your specific security requirements, we can help design the perfect multilayered solution to help keep your business safe.

WHAT CAN HIGH TOUCH DO TO HELP?

High Touch is well equipped to design, implement, and support cybersecurity requirements ranging from basic firewall installations to advanced HIPAA and PCI-compliant solutions.

Combining our IT and cybersecurity expertise, we help keep businesses safe. High Touch can offer a customized cybersecurity solution for your business
and/or technology consulting

services to help you uncover and understand your business's needs.

CONCLUSION

Cybersecurity is important because it protects you or your company from potential cyber threats. The advancement of technology has left many people vulnerable to cybercriminal activities, such as hacking, data theft and damage, and industrial espionage. Cybercrime rate is increasing; hence, without cyber security, you could lose sensitive information, money, or reputation. Cyber security is as important as the need for technology.

www.ingramcontent.com/pod-product-compliance
Ingram Content Group UK Ltd.
Pitfield, Milton Keynes, MK11 3LW, UK
UKHW021658190726
13853UKWH00001B/331

9 798494 559869